Reinstated 7/86

The Mexican Night

—Travel Journal—

Ferlinghetti

· A New Directions Paperbook

Library of Congress Catalog Card Number: 75-122105

ACKNOWLEDGMENTS
Some of these entries previously appeared in City Lights Journal, Evergreen Review, The San Miguel Review and El Corno Emplumado.

First published as New Directions Paperbook 300 in 1970

Published simultaneously in Canada by McClelland & Stewart Limited. Manufactured in the United States of America

New Directions Books are published for James Laughlin by New Directions Publishing Corporation, 333 Sixth Avenue, New York 10014

for
Lorenzo
should he someday
come upon himself
in that labyrinth
of solitude

April 22–27, 195?

Pardon me if I disappear in Mexico, wearing a mask and strange suspenders. Puncho Villa. Wandering about, speaking my curious 'spagnol. The trees are coming down, we'll to the woods no more, mad mind and black sun, we'd better find an island quick. Though there's no longer any "away." Southbound through the Toltec debris, the dark horse still a free runner. Under what volcano. . . . My soul in various pieces and I attempting to reassemble it, mistaking bird cries for ecstatic song when they are really cries of despair. And poetry a precession of waterbirds in flight mixed with motor accidents, o drunk flute o golden mouth, flower in the bunghole, kiss kiss in stone boudoirs. Voice lost & dreaming, door floated over the horizon. Where am I? Leaving Alamos on a local heap of a bus, full of vaqueros in hard cowboy hats, smoking Sonora Gold on the back seats, stoned blind in the dusk. One hombre passes me a huge joint, size of a Brown Bomber. Setting yellow sun slants through the bus. Gone now. . . . Thus did he see first the dark land. . . . Dark trees flash by, white leaves nested in them like birds. . . .

FERLINGHETTI. 1961

'Lower' California

October 24, 1961

A visionary journey without visions, in a stone blind land—the new Mexico still the Old Beat Mexico—that huge dark foodshit smell still here (which I first smelled in dank woodwork of a Mexico City pension, 1939). . . . In Ensenada, on the blank Pacific, there's always a wind full of sand at this season, and you don't get The Smell on the long dustcrud street by the bay—but stick your head in some cantina and you get it, full in the nose. . . . Ensenada, Baja California—bah on this baja—who stole the sun? where's love? Brown Hades! Dig the native habitations, groin streets, mud people. Only the kids and dogs have anything left in them—and the dogs can't stand it—they lie around stretched out with flies all over them in the gutters, a curious race apart. I saw one dunghill dog go in a church, up the center aisle, looking for his *pugh* (that's a smelly pun) he scooted out a side door quick, no place for him in there, he scared maybe by the wood confessionals like doorless phone booths where priests sat listening to penitents on each side hidden in curtains, each by a little lattice window through which whispers

went— Priest listened to both at once, answered both at once, or confused the two? Were those phoners getting thru to any Central? Daddy, I've been disconnected. Stagger out into the dust land. Perhaps I could learn to love this land if I stayed awhile—tho it's the third or fourth time I've been to Mex already— If Los Angeles is the Asshole of America, what is this brown appendage down here? Lost Ensenada, existing only by the force of gravity—stuck in the earth forever. . . .

. . . I arrived at night, on a creaking bus, among devious faces. In the morning, all's different. There's palm trees and sun, streetsweepers are out, sprinklers go by to lay the dust, the bay is calm with fishing boats, mountains rise up. . . .

The day before in Tijuana—I walked around with McGilvery and Floy Damon from LaJolla, digging the jumbled streets, eating roast corn from street-vendors, drinking Cervesa under arbors in back gardens of crazy hillside restaurants, stopping to watch local celebration at Mexican Lions Club of United Nations Day— A little Mexican municipal band struck up its mournful flourish when officials arrived in open limousines, an enormous racket of trumpets and trombones and drums sounding as if some truck had just blown its muffler. It's a full minute before the blowers get together on the tune—and stumble on into the Blue Danube. A dead dog lay on its side by the entrance, flies in his eyes, up his nose—the Lion that didn't make it.

October 25

Hotel Plaza, Ensenada (town without a plaza), room on roof I look two ways out of, to sea and mountain, over flat rooftop town— I hear roosters before dawn, see the light growing, headlights of junkheap cars coming down hillside, a little brown bird on windowsill seems about to take off—no, it's a tiny halfbuilt house with frame of roof like wings on top of hill outlined against first windowlight. . . . Up before dawn, writing, I'm some faroff hungup Hemingway character waking in some small Spanish hotel alone, counting my marbles. Or the ghost of Elliot Paul contemplating the life & death of a Spanish town. I see myself ten years ago in Majorca, in Andraitx port, lost fishing village, where they fished up those mute Phoenician urns. . . . From which way will the fascists come this time, baby? I can almost hear their minutemen machineguns in San Diego. . . . *Can I survive another transplantation?*

I ride on the beach on a brown horse, rented from a caballero called Alfonso. Horse is called Elefanto. Alfonso rides along on his horse singing a slow Indian song, points out a stucco shack beyond the dunes where he has two wives. We gallop past. Dusk is falling, night creeps up out of sea. A gaggle of dark fishermen struggles past onto a pier with nets; under great hats like turtle shells, they scuttle into dark ocean: the distance between man and primeval mud measured from below sea level.

October 27

Three days here, and I can't stand it any longer, I'll leave in the morning. Dirt streets of shitcity! It's like dying; suppose there were no escape—yet the people here smile at each other from time to time & act as if they still had some great slur of hope somewhere. While consuls drink themselves to death. Help! *No se puede vivir sin amar?* Let the ocean come in and cover it.

October 28

Ensenada to Tijuana to Mexicali by bus. Rode all day, contemplating the earth, saw nothing. Endless riprap roads, hills, mountains, hopeless houses, trees, sagebrush, fences, dust, burros, dry land. Dry people stuck to it. . . . Passing thru Tijuana, I see legless man at downtown dirt corner sitting in backseat of antique sedan from which doors have been torn. He has stained felt hat on center of head, rimless eyeglasses with cracked glass, a huge old typewriter propped up before him on wood box. Typing, he has butt of cigarette stuck to lower lip, burnt-out. Signs hung on car say

ESCRITOR PUBLICO

A campesino is speaking to him from the curb, he writes what he hears; a great writer, this here Public Stenographer, Public Writer giving people back true images of themselves. Legless, he holds the mirror up. . . .

Tijuana to Mexicali, approaching town of Tecate, bus passes thru hill country strewn thickly with rocks from road to horizon, nothing but rocks, rocks, millions of them covering the landscape, in place of trees. Nature has tried everything! There's beautiful country further on, other side of Tecate—rock mountains, Tibetan peaks (one of those border mountains north of Tecate, on U.S. side, inhabited by American translator

of the *Tibetan Book of the Dead*). We roll on between hills of small rocks, pepper trees and sage and twisted fir growing out of rockhills, rock mountains beyond, sunset coming, bright sun flames close over, bright blue sky with rock holes in it, whole fantastic mountainous landscape of nothing but stone. Then suddenly, at turn of highway high up, a great dry brown plain stretched way below, Eastward and Northward for a hundred miles, North America. . . .

Arrived at Mexicali, another dust town, only worse, in midst of flat brown plain I saw from above, at nightfall—bus station crammed with campesinos looking grim, tough & hungry, under enormous hats & ponchos, waiting for country busses and revolutions. These are the Front Teeth of Latin America. . . . I walk out into mud boulevard & vision of utter Desolation, Dung & Death in the image of crowded streets and dark people. Everywhere I walk & look, the same! Enough to drive any voyeur back home. . . . Later, found the tourist part of town, and the American border: big sign over it saying UNITED STATES. Showed my California Driver's license and went thru to the American Zone, saw an American movie with Bingo advertised with double feature. Went in. Bingo just starting, American on stage with mike announcing numbers drawn out of whirling basket, says numbers in American and in atrocious Spanish. . . . Came out at midnight, walked back thru border station, no one on Mexican side to check—completely open in

that direction. Sign said in English: "Narcotics Addicts
& Users Are Required by U.S. Law to Register Before
Leaving Country." Also: "Warning: Cats & Dogs
Leaving U.S. May Not Be Allowed to Re-enter."
Do not pee on the wrong side of the fence. Show your
dogtags. Borders must be maintained! An insane
fluidity & deracination surely would prevail without
them—no countries, no nations, nothing at all to stop
us anywhere, nothing to stop the hordes of the world
still starving and howling like Calibans at the gates,
no customs, no wars, no protective tariffs, no passports,
no immigration and naturalization papers, none of
the old protective barriers protecting everyone from
everyone else, even the oceans dried up eventually,
leaving us no alternative but to recognize Indians
as brothers, the whole earth only one continent,
under it all, after all, all colors of skin at length
blended into one skin with one tongue. It'll only take
5000 more years to do this, Indian, even after wasting
2000 mostly in the wrong direction. A very simple
little revolution could accomplish it in no time: declare
an immediate moratorium on all liaisons, partnerships,
and marriages between all people of the same color,
everyone immediately to seek union with someone
of a different color, all national flags made into snotrags
or bandages to be used in maternity hospitals giving
birth to nothing but a new generation of babies of
nothing but mixed colors & races. . . . In the meantime,
I wander about the landscape, making like that

American Indian whom Henry Miller wished to have at his side when he crossed the continent in his unconditioned *Nightmare,* the one he wanted to have with him when he viewed the smoking steel mills by roadbeds of Pittsburgh in an *Inferno* Dante never dreamed of. I am ready to return to the Cave at any moment, carry a flint arrowhead in my pocket, just in case. Cro-magnons carried stones for books.

October 29

My last night in Mexico I spend in Mexican border hotel overlooking the wire barricades. This hotel advertises "Clima Artificial"—but the air-conditioned night in Mexico is different—the Clima Artificial doesn't work. In the middle of the night I tear open my hermetically sealed window which is about the size of my head. A fine dust sifts in from the street. . . .

I sit writing this in the pay toilet of the Greyhound station in Calisco, across the border again next morning. Suddenly my 16¢ ballpoint pen slips from my fingers and falls down into the john. Here I make a grave mistake. I flush it, hoping to clear the muddy waters and retrieve my stylo. When the waters clear, my stylo is gone, forever. Perhaps it will reappear centuries later in the alluvia of the Rio Grande, and some strange-colored descendant of Americans come upon it, wondering what strange weapon is this, and how many it killed with what ammunition. Words?
So drowns my Journal.

The Road To Topolobampo

I owe to such evenings the idea I have of innocence.
—Albert Camus*

May, 1962.

Sitting at a table in the Parke de la Cruz Blanca,
Chihuahua, Sunday afternoon, bright sun . . . I write
in a marble notebook with rainbow edges,

We were born
under the mulberry trees
From which drop
the mynah birds of madness.

Someone is playing an accordian, it is Sunday in a
Seurat garden.

Fish float
thru the trees
Eating the seeds
of the sun . . .

The crowd I came with has gone back to Las
Cruces. I've two days to wait for the train, to
Topolobampo. I walk around town, aimlessly. A
storm is coming, sky clouding, wind rising. I lie on my
back in the middle of another park, a great grassy
park full of willows & palm trees & fountains. Couples

* Italics in the first part of these notes are from Camus'
Myth of Sisyphus (Knopf, 1955)

lie scattered on the grass, as in a pointillist painting, dappled. Laughter muffled. Pieces of voices drift by. I see the tops of the palms shaking, with huge swishing noises, sweeping the sky. Yet the wood clouds do not move. High school boys come by joking & tumbling behind the circular bandstand. "Imbeciles in neckties drop from the trees." The ghost of Malcolm Lowry skulks from behind a bush carrying his sign:

Le Gusta Este Jardin?
Que Es Suyo?
Evite Que Sus Hijos Lo Destruyan!
. . . etcetera.

In coal night, black train starts up at last, noiseless. Reaches Westward for the Sierra Madre, upward. Thru black solitudes, green nowheres with the light turned off. **Au pays du Tarahumara,** that wild junkie landscape Artaud apprehended. Still I'm not with him, I'm with Camus who also rushed too fast into his unknown, in this **cama alta**. . . . In this upper berth of being, there is a slight noiseless rocking, as of the universe, and we advance only in darkness, no windows upon the mescal landscape, a bunker in space. In such night of earth, *the unreasonable silence of the world returns,* night a kind of barbaric tongue-tied mongoloid sphinx who will never speak. No answers there! *The primitive hostility of the world rises up to face us across the millennia.* Thru it, we dream onward, skull blind. Wrapped in our own skins.
It is an old story.

Suplicamos
QUIETUD
En Beneficio de los que ya
Descansan

I am indebted to the young German playwright Gunter Eich whose radio play applied the image of the closed train (hurtling faster and faster thru night) to the postwar German situation—a boxcar with an old couple & a couple of kids closed in, hurled to an unknown destination thru a landscape the young have never seen and the elders find impossible to describe. . . . *The world comes to a stop but also lights up.* Our consciousness is the projector, the moment of attention, which focuses on successive images, and each is a truth yet there's no Truth discernible as a whole. Consciousness is merely the act of attention; it understands nothing in itself. There's *no scenario, but a successive and coherent illustration.*

My projector is being hurled thru the dark. If my mind is strong enough I can liken it to one of those cyclops searchlights mounted on flatcars, piercing the sky yet reaching only so far and no farther, no matter how powerful. Fortunately I do not have that kind of mind. I have a flickering little halfass projector that must resort to all sorts of improvisations in order to function. And no live God discoverable except consciousness itself. And that consciousness itself an improvisation, a drug or a dream. So that, passing thru the stoned country of the Tarahumaras, we

continuously improvise our existence, make up our lives as we go, improvise our present, our future, make up our own Topolobampo.

Topolobampo itself is a bleary little fishing port on the Pacific, one of those rag ends of native civilization, half in ruins, harbor like a lost pocket in a canvas poncho, ringed with strange barren islands and lonely juttings of Topolobampo Bay. The road from Los Mochis (flyspecked inland Tortilla Flat) ends suddenly at the base of one small treeless hill, and by a bumpy stone rut one passes up and around to the main pier at the foot of the center of the town which fills the seaward side of the hill and leans over it almost into the water. Two or three small rusty coasters are tied up at the pier like stranded cockroaches.

Ragged hollering urchins of all sizes are running and jumping and swimming off the dock and off the lee side of one of the listing cockroaches, the dark water at least twenty feet below stirred with great splashes and wriggling bodies as in some flailing shipwreck at sea, tattered cries echoing.

Above, in the town itself, screenless, glassless shacks & houses stare down, everything open, as in some Italian hillside village, with a tiny plaza no bigger than the inside of a stone church, the people barefoot, itching with **chinchas,** sitting on beat-up open terraces or in big bare swing-door bars hanging from the

hillside. And the whole dive creeping with babies, brats of all ages, teen-age **muchachas** (already women) in torn cotton shifts laughing & chattering, mud-hut whores among them, and old fishermen sitting silent with grandmothers in shawls like reaper deaths. Sundown, 1962. Come back in 1972 and it'll be transformed with gringo hotels on the waterfront, stucco cafes, guides, post cards, pluribus dollars. The railroad just opened from Chihuahua will see to all that.

There's an Indian fishing village on one of the islets in the bay which is also being considered. . . .

•

The road to Topolobampo runs ten miles south-southwest in a straight line from Los Mochis. There is a **camion** that runs every half hour or whenever the driver wants to travel. I take one of these jitneys a little before sunset. It is filled to bursting with: two or three young hombres in huge hats, a couple of old hags in kerchiefs, several mothers and little boys and girls, babies in slings, baskets, wicker birdcages, shopping bags, burlap bags, and an ancient phonograph and a stand-up microphone carried by one of the men in sombreros, the whole works jammed into four rows of sprung seats. At the helm, the **chofer** is a young cat with the usual sexy little Latin moustache. As soon as he gets off the dirt streets and dust riprap of Los Mochis and onto the paved one-lane highway to Topolobampo he turns the radio on full blast with **mariachi** music and relaxes. He's a **mancarron,** a

one-armed man, but still is able to wave his arm about in great gesticulations & oaths any time any animal happens to get in his way on the road. There's a little lace fringe strung along the top of the windshield to shade the eyes from the sun, there's a metal creche and a plastic madonna in a little metal altar stuck to the top of the dashboard so that, sitting in the back, low down, you look thru holy objects to see the road and the horizon way beyond. Later, more than one peak sticks out of the flat plain, but for most of the ten-mile straightaway you see this one peak rising up at the very end of the road at the very end-point of the endless perspective, and, looking back, you see another very similar cone-shaped peak rising up behind Los Mochis. Between these two weird cones runs this perfectly arrowlike narrow highway upon which the setting sun, yellow-red, streams, the **camion** seeming hardly to progress down that long perspective, even as it rocks along steadily to the howling of the robot radio tuned to one of those crazy Mexican stations emitting a hilarious mixture of dramatic advertisements for shoes, American jazz played by violins and cornets, church bells thrown in to punctuate special announcements, sexy male announcers sounding as if they were simultaneously seducing a housewife and reporting a fire in the studio, all mixed together with **mariachis** (who must be kept handy at the station at all hours to be thrown in like shock troops whenever the slightest threat of silence presents itself).

Or maybe it is all only a recording of life, played over & over, the whole trip like some weird little record or film running on & on, some kind of comatose dream in which the film withers and slips and the **camion** keeps rolling forever on and on into the **sol poliente** and into the infinitely narrowing perspective, yet does not advance, everyone strangely silent, all together listening absently and intently to the crazy outpourings of the radio tuned to the world, and digging the sad marcescent landscape of trees, huts, **campesinos,** slatterns at windows (cow-eyes stare out), donkeys, dogs, dry land, sea where coelacanths swim. . . .

It is **innocence,** it is their seeming **innocence** which presents itself incessantly, as you see the **camion** passengers so gravely taking in everything the hotrod announcer throws at them (The announcer himself knowing just whom he's talking to, in fact can see them all in every country backstreet in dustbin Mexico). He's talking to them in person, and they are listening, laughing, smiling, gawking out windows, peering ahead thru Madonna fringe as radio blasts on with rock-and-roll played by nothing but trumpets borrowed from hockshops in Mexico City (**monte de piedads** of leftover life). And the whole absurd Gestalt of the **camion** bowling along like some flippy total caravanserai-symbol, wheeling into space with all the ancient trappings, shawls & superstitions, hunger & flocked beauty (the young dark girl's eyes on the road)

carrying along with it all the claptraps and fandanglements of microphones, phonographs, plastic madonnas.

All sit there still groping on into the falling dusk. Innocence persists, insanely intarissable, in spite of all. The road does not end. It is as if the radio were not playing at all. There is a stillness in the air, in the light of the dusk, in the eyes fixed forward, in the still end of life, an intolerable sweetness. . . .

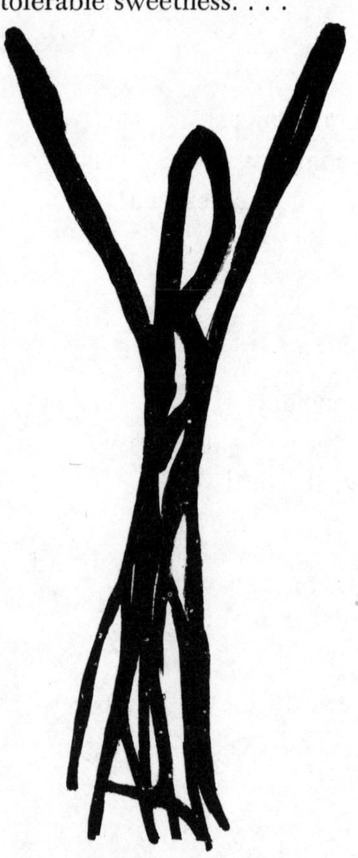

Cinqo de Mayo, 1962

Passing strange mountains
        & dropping pine needles
                in an envelope
I send you
        some of my bones. . . .

6 Mayo '62

Morning mocks its flowers
        by becoming
                Afternoon

7 Mayo '62

We have our moments
                of ecstasy
        and then the bird
                falls into
                        the absurd. . . .

Oaxaca

6 Sept. '68

Mad, a hole in my shoe, under the jacaranda trees and the great Indian laurels, roots still in the Ganges, in the plaza de Oaxaca. . . . And then at night by the circular bandstand listening to the marimba music, everyone out strolling or on the park benches in the semi-dark, the high lamps shining through the trees. . . . A wandered statue myself . . . where my pedestal?

Mitla

7 Sept.

"Jesus mio misericordia"—one of those Bleeding Christ churches one stumbles into in all the small sad towns of adobe Mexico: entered at 13 minutes after 12 noon & dropped a big copper Mexican penny into the plaster box held by a 5-foot-high plaster altar-boy at the side entrance, startled by the big clunking noise the coin made as it fell through the false bottom of the plaster box & down through the plaster statue itself into a hollow wooden stand upon which the statue stood—the heavy coin hitting the hollow wood base with a loud empty thud. Inside, not one but three bloody bleeding Christs—one stretched out under a garden-green trestle like a birdcage—not a trestle but a sort of bier with handles at each end and a cage of green bars over it—like some kind of stretcher used at sports events to carry victims off the field, take me out coach I've had it, your turn on the gridiron baby, your turn on that cross, what's these nail holes in me hands, fer Christ's sakes? This Christ not more than five-feet-long, with wood head and hands, stretched out under a white muslin sheet, only his head with

crown of thorns showing—like an invalid in bed asleep, blood on the forehead & the lips dripping with it, the green bier trestle like some garden-house trellis with white & blue paper flowers strung on paper vines over His Head; and on the side of the bier in handwritten scrawl—"Jesus mio misericordia." . . . Stumble out into the sun, daddy, and make it among the Mexican tourists just disgorged from a tour-bus, blinking through sunglasses & cameras. . . .

Oaxaca

Night of Sept. 7

Corner of Avenida de l'Independencia in front of the Science Institute of the University of Oaxaca just off the main plaza, a student revolutionary rally going on in the floodlighted little square with a wooden speaker's stand set up, the front of the Instituto hung with huge cloth & cardboard signs: TIERRA Y LIBERTAD, OLYMPIAD DE HAMBRE, VIVA LA JUVENTAD, A LA VICTORIA POR EL ESPIRITU JOVEN Y LA ACCION REVOLUTIONARIA, LIBERTAD DE ESTUDIANTES PRESOS, EL GOBIERNO LLAMA LEY A SU PROPIA VIOLENCIA, HASTA LA VICTORIA SIEMPRE–VENCEREMOS. The square filled with standing townspeople, dark and quiet but not hostile, listening to the shouted speeches bounced off the walls by gravelly loudspeakers, the student speakers fired up, gesticulating into the microphone, crying out great revolutionary phrases into the Oaxacan night, dense Indian dark. . . . And around the corner, squatted against a wall of the Institute, just out of the floodlight, across the street from a big bank, a blind guitar player squatting in the dust, playing & singing

very quietly in the semi-dark of that side-street, his steady low voice an undertone beneath the shouted political voices, the end of his guitar wrapped in torn plastic, he picking at the guitar with a sure calm lively rhythm, his voice going on & on, chipped white enamel tin cup, empty, clamped between his knees, beneath another sign: PUEBLO UNETE A TUS HERMANOS. Applause for the speakers, the singer's cup empty. He's bearded but not old, his straw sombrero on the ground next to him, he barefoot, ragged all over, with calm handsome face, maybe part Indian but not much, his low voice clear & strong & calm under all, his gut-string guitar going on & on, below the shouted speeches, below the radical resolutions, beneath the eternal cries for Progress & Liberty, across from the bank, on the ground, hermano, not exactly "united" with the pueblo, yet he its old voice under all, behind & under all, still coming through, sounding through, he's like part of the tierra, rooted in that earth, the song going on under the night, his voice coming in again & again under the speeches, like some kind of revolutionary rejoinder, echo & contretemps, answer to all, the guitar driving on under his voice. People come & go, crowd applauds, cars roar down the side-streets blowing dust in his face, shined shoes brush his dirty feet, and his song goes on, no part of him moving but his strum hand on the guitar, a full moon above winging thru the clouds, no expression on its face or his, as his voice comes thru

again in a pause between speeches. His head is cocked to one side now, as if he were even listening to the speeches the whole time. And answering. 1968: Year of the Mexican Olympics: "Olympiad de Hambre." Olympic of Hunger. . . .

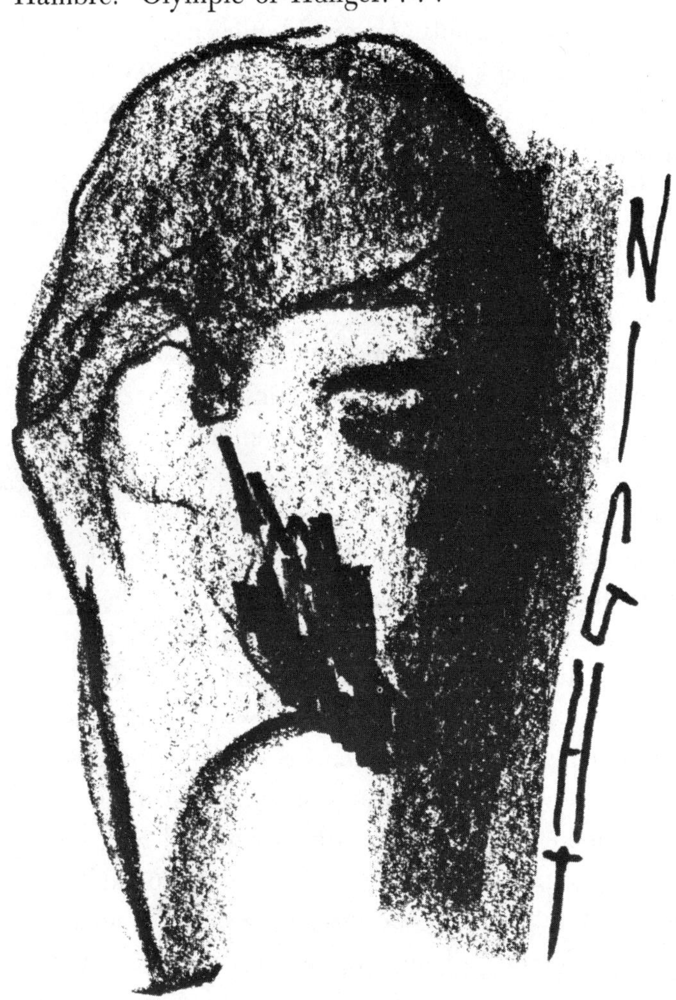

Tues. Sept. 10

Shoe cauchemar in the streets of Mexico City– millions of shoes, tongues agape, coming at me, a sea of soles flapping–all Latin American countries curiously filled with millions & millions of shoe-freaks– Ever notice how many shoestores there are per block in Mexico City or Havana or Lima Peru? Or La Paz Bolivia? . . . . I am wandering thru the Zocalo, Mexico monster city, past the Monte de Piedad (National Pawnshop) and across the enormous plaza at midday, & here come the millions of shoes, tongues in all of them, dusty in the burning sun, all kinds of them, all shapes & sizes, coming past me & past the Monte de Piedad with its national hopes in hock & revolutions in pawn; then on thru the twobillion fourmillion city, down the great boulevards, Avenida Hidalgo, Avenida Juarez, and the Alameda Central, great central park, hot in the afternoon siesta sun, no siesta, señor, but noon nightmare streets & shoes filled with foreign feet, on sticks in pants & skirts, faces fixed to the upper ends of them, pouring past me where I sit on a wrought-iron bench in a corner of the great park, and then the traffic flooding round me later where I stand on an island in the middle of Avenida Juarez, trying to snare an impossible taxi, all full, all careening thru the massed screaming traffic, pedestrians crossing against all the lights, brakes screeching, horns stuck, me too swimming in the crowds from island to island, shoes

a-flap, where am I going? Suddenly a sharp cobblestone strikes through my left shoe sole & the forgotten beginning of a hole, and I understand in a dumb flash how revolutions die on foot, die afoot—a shoe wears through and falls apart a long way from home—foot soldiers limp onward—a donkey needs reshoeing—a guerrilla camion wears its tires bald & there are no spares—Ché Guevara ties together his shredded boots & goes on, shifts to rough sandals, *abarcas,* and staggers on thru the jungle. . . . The city jungle at midday just as thick & hot, full of just as many hallucinations, noon nightmares & lost tongues. The shoes come at me, all tongueless now. And the big hole now in the bottom of my left shoe, only my right shoe now capable of effective action, the second stage of any revolution when it is easier to go to the Right than further Left. My kingdom for a horse? Nevermind the horse, nevermind the hole in my soul. . . . I go to the occupied University of Mexico campus in late afternoon—with some poets and editors of "El Corno Emplumado"—and pass through the barricades into the buildings held by the students, like Cuba 1960 with young cats in fatigues guarding the entrances & chicks with rifles. A calm prevails today. In the Med School the students have embalmed the bodies of some of their comrades killed by the government of the people. The army is a mile away, cooling it for the olympics. Soon it will happen. It does. Still Ché Guevara goes on, through the jungles. . . .

The Mind of Ché Guevara a Day After His Death

Sept. 11, '68

AH ACA LA VIDA GONDOLA PUERTA
ESCONDIDA REVOLUTIONARIA ACA PALMITO
ACA CHOCLOS ZAPALLOS YUCAS ACA CHACO
HAMBRE EL ELEVADOR ESCONDIDO AYMARAS
Y CAMBAS ACA ARMADILLO PERDIDO NO
REVOLUCIONARIO ACA TAPERAS PALMITOS
DE COROJO PERDIDAS TRANSPORTES DE
ANIMALES FORRAJES Y SEMILLAS ADONDE
ADONDE ESTAN   ADONDE ESTAN
GUARIJOS ADONDE ADONDE ESTAN
ADONDE ALEIDA ERNESTITO   CELIA
TANIA HILDA CELIA   CHICOS Y CHICAS
HERMANOS ADONDE EN ESTE CHILCHEO
NADA   NADA   NADA QUE CHANCHOS
TATUS NADA QUE NADA   CHILCHEO EN
CHUCHIAL Y DONDE DONDE ESTA DONDE
PACHUNGA Y DONDE ESTA BIGOTES Y DONDE
ESTA PAPI Y DONDE ESTANISLAO   NEGRO
ANTONIO JOAQUIN   APOLINAR
RICARDO CHINCHU   JORGE EL LORO

PACHO PACO PACHUNGO OLO VILO POLO
MORO MOROGORO MUNGA
MUGANGA Y EL MEDICO FELIX EL RUBIO
IVAN RENAN Y PEDRO PAN DIVINO
MAURICIO PAN DIVINO EL PELAO
CARLOS LUIS CHAPACO CAMPANEROS
CAMPANEROS GONDOLO
REVOLUCIONARIO TATU Y TANIA
Y CELIA Y ALEIDA Y ALEIDA
ERNESTITO NADA QUE CHOCLO
HUMINTA BAGRE SED Y HAMBRE JOCO
CHARQUI ADONDE ADONDE
GUARIJOS ZAPALLOS YUCAS HOCHIS
CARACORES CARACORES
CARACORES ANTAS CAMBAS
GUERILLAS YANQUIS
NADA QUE BOROS CHANCOS Y
CHINCHAS Y PULGAS CHINGA MI
MADRE CHINGA QUE QUE
PASA QUE PASA SENOR QUE
ES QUE PASA AQUI
TIENEN SED HAMBRE ADONDE
ADONDE CACARES CACARES CARAJO
NINGUN CACARES AHORA AQUI
AQUI AHORA ADONDE NO CHANKAKA NO
CACA NO CARACORE CHINGA
HAMBRE ADONDE CACARES NADA AQUI
NO SENTINAL RADIO BEMBA ABAJO EN
BARRANCO PIERDAS NO REVOLUCIONARIOS

PERO   PERO ESTAN ADONDE MIS
ABARCAS   ADONDE MIS BOTAS   SI
MIS BOTAS EN ELEVADOR SIEMPRE   ACA
ALLA   ALLI   VAMOS PA'LANTE
GRITA CACARE   MIS ABARCAS
LLEVALAS

PA'LANTE
SIEMPRE

MIS BOTAS
LLEVALAS
SIEMPRE
AL TERRITORIO LIBRE

AL TERRITORIO LIBRE

AQUI
ACA

PA'LANTE

Y

Y

GRITA

GRITA

CACARE

Grita Cacare? The birds still cry out: In 1970, from a 'Territoris Libre,' this message was to come from the editors of CORNO:

Concerning the Suppression of El Corno Emplumado

EL CORNO EMPLUMADO is a bi-lingual quarterly that for eight years from Mexico City reflected much of the struggle and pain and birth in Latin and North America. It was never backed by any official institution and it made available the work of hundreds of writers and artists, many in the youngest vanguard, for the first time. Its life was the constant struggle of any independent publication. By 1968, about a third of its economic base came from several Mexican government subsidies.

The student movement in Mexico, gaining strength and unity in its fight against exploitation by a government that only serves the interests of its own ruling class and its U.S. imperialist masters, was hit a decisive blow on October 2, 1968, when approximately 500 students and citizens attending a peaceful meeting in the Tlatelolco Plaza were surrounded by special government troops and murdered. It was ten days before the Olympic Games were to open in Mexico City. The gov-

ernment got rid of "unsightly trouble" with hundreds of deaths and several thousand more in prison (from July through October). The city was hung with colorful flags and balloons and the white dove of peace—official Olympic symbol. Citizens threw red paint at the white doves. In EL CORNO EMPLUMADO #28 we vigorously protested the repression, as well as the misery and oppression which is the life of a majority of Mexicans.

All magazines in Mexico that dared to cry out against these events immediately suffered withdrawal of subsidy. Most of them were in that way easily prevented from appearing. El Corno made a widespread appeal for help among poets, readers, other editors and friends, and the response was such that the next issue came out right on time, protesting as strongly as its predecessor, and including letters from two of the new political prisoners. Following this, a new and independent publishing house, MOVIMIENTO EDITORES, offered to take on publication of our magazine. (Our association with them, through our last two successful issues, has had to be terminated because of the events described below; but back issues may still be obtained from them at Zamora 70, Colonia Condesa, Mexico 11, DF).

Issues #30 and #31 clearly demonstrated our position as a revolutionary magazine. Number 31 appeared on July 1st. On July 7th, we received a visit in our home from an agent disguising himself as an investigator from the Mexican Social Security Institute. With a complaint concerning the alleged operation of a sewing shop(!) in our home, he was able to enter our house. Using agile and sly methods of deception, he was able to obtain Margaret's Mexican passport. He escaped in a waiting unmarked car, its motor running and two men inside it.

We denounced the theft in the local police station

(legal procedure required in Mexico preliminary to issuance of new document) and applied for a replacement. It was promised for eight days later, eight days during which the same agent returned once when we were not at home and called several times. When Margaret went to pick up her new passport she was informed that there were "irregularities" and it couldn't be issued. At that very moment there were armed and uniformed agents at our house, and their visits were to continue for several weeks. But we, and our four children, never went back home.

The following weeks included sending the kids out of the country for their safety and our mobility—and the beginning of a series of useless official (through a lawyer) and extra-official (through friends) attempts to obtain a document which in Mexico is "every citizen's right." Several times the agents and/or police who visited the house and threatened the people watching it mentioned our magazine. An article was published in the local press announcing the death of the publication, but still the government seemed intent on keeping Margaret in the country.

[. . . . .], a government official, was approached by a group of writers asking that the passport be granted and calling for an end to harrassment. His only answer was "It's a very difficult problem," this response coming the same week in which he had stated, concerning the case of two students who had hijacked a plane to Cuba for political reasons, that "every citizen of this country has the constitutional right to a passport and free travel."

Another official [. . . . .], was visited by Margaret herself. He expressed no knowledge of the case while demonstrating the opposite, claimed that he would "look into it," and settled back to mastermind other forms of government repression. It seems clear that both [of these officials] (as well as many in the

Mexican government) work with or at the very least actively cooperate with the U.S. Central Intelligence Agency. Related evidence was uncovered by a recent spy scandal (when an official of the Mexican embassy in Cuba was exposed as a CIA operative); and who else could create such "a very difficult problem" . . . or an insoluble affair for [these officials], but that Northern boss holding the reigns on so much of Latin America?

Why do we feel the repression in our case took this form? Why the robbery of the passport? We had been planning to live and work in Cuba for several years, and our Fall travel plans were more or less common knowledge. The Mexicans should have been glad to get rid of us. But the Americans never care to let their revolutionaries out of range, away from their control. And American control in Mexico is probably better than at home.

After almost three months of this situation . . . we decided to get out in whatever way we could, and so we did.

Students, who tried to observe the first anniversary of last year's bloody events, were being arrested even as we crossed the border. The repression we have suffered is nothing next to what has been happening to other brothers and sisters in Mexico. And the repression is not limited to the student sector: it's on all levels, everywhere. The air is on fire, the silence is temporary and misleading. People are not forgetting; they are preparing themselves for a long, hard fight. *A victorious fight!*

WE WILL WIN!

POWER TO THE PEOPLE!

LONG LIVE THE WORLD REVOLUTION!

—Margaret Randall & Robert Cohen
January, 1970

Guadalajara

7 Marzo '69 Revolucion Directo

Up and out early, into the bright plaza, first morning, white sun flares into plaza and park, church on plaza rings its skinny bell, a man hands me a free newspaper, a heavy bell tolls in another church of the same religion, the traffic flows through the middle of the long plaza, an avenue put right through the middle of it since I was here ten years ago to the month, quiet little square transformed into a downtown thoroughfare; still the birds sing in the high trees, twitter in the jacarandas. And the trees dance. . . . A beat-up bus made in 1917 full of dark workers, mostly Indios, creaks through the plaza, its destination-sign reading REVOLUCION DIRECTO. One doesn't have to wait long for this bus to that Plaza on mornings like this. I jump on, then jump off and run into two churches, one on each side of the avenue, mass going on in both of them, under the high stone naves and the gilt, only a half a dozen old women in there, in their black shawls, kneeling, but the service goes on, the priests and their acolytes making their eternal holy mumble; in the first church the wall behind the altar is maybe 100 feet high, completely gold-

plated, with maybe 15 life-size statues of old dead saints in niches at various levels up to the ceiling itself encrusted with flying sainted creatures. I mumble obscenities and rush out and into the second church. Same mass going on & on. In a side aisle is a glass-enclosed bier, and inside lies the statue of a dead monk or Christ himself on a trip, eyes open, hands folded. Down by his feet lies an old skull, eye-sockets gaping out of the sixteenth century, and for some reason there is a brass ring affixed in the top of the head. For some reason! To swing the Cat from heaven, to hook him back up to heaven when life on planet is finished, to swing from the top of the huge high dusty nave above the altar on a long string, like a pendulum, swinging slowly the whole vast and terrible distance in the upper air over the pews, like a huge clapper, clapping for God, a real swinger. I rush out and grab the next bus marked REVOLUCION DIRECTO. . . . I am sitting in the back, toying with my skull, eye-sockets staring out at the massed humanity on crowded avenidas, awaiting *its* bus along the route of Hidalgo's March for Freedom. In the bus everyone is smoking cigars, and I see now they are not Indios at all; they have been transformed into *mestizos*, and now they are all diplomats in morning coats, and they are blowing their noses on various flags. The most popular flag for this purpose seems to be North American. One diplomat is even using one to wipe up the semen he has just succeeded in

ejaculating. Some of it has even gotten into his good eye, and he is using the flag of the United States of North America like a pocket handerchief, dabbing at his eye with it, and I am not so sure he is not crying, for this is a political-parapsychological parable, and there is as much salt in semen as in tears. A star falls out of the flag, and I pick it up and put it in my pocket. I can always use an extra state. I notice now that it is not an American flag at all which this particular star has fallen out of; it's the flag of some small Latin American mañana republic, and the stars weren't sewn on too well, which I as an Americano del Norte was the first to notice. There may be other used stars to be picked up at bargain prices. New Mexico was cheap enough, practically nada, but the loose stars on the flags on this bus may prove even cheaper, the bus fare being cheap enough if you've got real money rather than these perishable paper pesos and other misery-notes. The diplomat who didn't even notice me pocketing his star now is engaged in wiping the eyes of the bus driver who is an Indio with shades in a vaquero hat. He keeps singing out "Gracias, señor!" and hurtles the bus onward, displaying his *machismo,* through the crooked city streets which seem to have gotten narrower and narrower and more and more crowded all the time as the centuries wheel by. The bus itself gets absolutely jammed with citizens hanging out all the windows and onto the sides. There is one cripple who can walk

only on all-fours, but he now succeeds in keeping up with the bus and hollering epithets at it, for the bus now has to go so slow through the crowds. Every once in a while this deformed creature raises up and sticks his so-called face through a bus window, right into mine. He has a small monkey on his back, and the monkey carries a small parrot, and the parrot has a small jade stone in its mouth, and the parrot screams at everyone in Portuguese, which is the language of all good parrots, according to a guidebook I am reading on Revolucion, noting also that the "second language" of all good parrots is Spanish, no matter what dictator they are living with, and that to try to teach them anything else like Russian is useless, even an adulteration. The last time the monkey swings the parrot into the bus marked Revolucion, the bird jumps off and perches on the driver's head, and the driver starts using the parrot's voice, calling out the various localities and way-stations through which it seems we are passing, followed by names of Mexican or Indian or Latin American heroes that happened to pop into his weird head, much in the following manner: "Calle Constitucion! Juarez! Zapata! Hidalgo!" The bus now becomes so crowded that the diplomats in their swallowtail coats now have at least one campesino or Indio or beggar or vaquero sitting in their laps, and there are a few old crones thrown in on top of all, cackling and toothless in their shredded shawls, some carrying babies wrapped in flags. The diplomats have

now taken to picking each others' noses, and there is now also quite a bit of backward fellatio going on between the old crones, who turn out not to be so old as all that, and the diplomats, who turn out not to be so young as all that. Every once in a while a diplomat lets go of his diploma and lets out a curious cry and zips up his fly and then proceeds to mop up again with his flag. I look down now and see that my own flag, I mean my own fly, is open, and a huge snake now raises its head out of it, and looks directly at me, winking its one eye. It has a jade head. The bus suddenly careens to a fullstop in front of some Latin American embassy or national hockshop, and a flock of gaviotas flies up pronto out of a cupola and lets go with a shower of guano on the busload of revolutionists & hangers-on. The flags are pressed into service spontaneously in a new great mopping-up operation gumshoe. While this is in progress, a very *macho* Madonna of Revolucion flies or falls out of a stained-glass window into my lap. I proceed to introduce her to my snake. "It won't bite!" I tell her. But it does. And when I squirm out of my striped pants to really screw her, I notice the stripes are no longer Red White & Blue, and my top hat with the Red White & Blue stars & stripes is suddenly blown away over the heads of the cheering crowds still now rushing together at last in every Plaza de Revolucion where a bearded man whose name is not Quetzalcoatl mounts the wooden stage. . . .

Uxmal, Or the Flight to the Sun

March ’69

At Uxmal, in the rain forest, I am climbing up a great unfinished pyramid, its base hidden in jungle. Through the mouth of the rain-god Chac I entered the Pyramid of the Magician and now climb up & up, dragging a huge basket of stones for the construction of the pyramid. I am wearing a loincloth and a hat of pineapple leaves. My skin is dark brown with green tints, and it glistens with rivulets of sweat. The sun beats down from directly above the pyramid where it seems to be stuck in the meridian. The stones I am carrying are round as sun-stones and do not stay in place when I get them at last to the top of the pyramid. They go rolling down the stone steppes of the pyramid, like stone eggs. I climb down and begin over. It is another day and the sun is rising again over the pyramid. My basket is full of sun-stones, and they are incised with curious circular calendars. The sun turns in its white sky like the loose wheel of some sun-chariot. I crawl higher with my sun-stones, place them on the top, at last, and lie down on top, with a jade stone in my mouth. The sun itself rolls down on

top of me, spinning. It is made of peyote and white hot sperm, jism of the universe. I am a part of "Space Odyssey 2001" but I am also a bloodshot Indian maid being impregnated by a bronze Indian prince seven feet tall. The white hot sperm falls in showers. The moon rises and drenches us in pulverized peyote. The jade stone, which had been destined to be set at the very tip of the pyramid, is still on my tongue as I suddenly stretch my arms and take off into the sun, to catch the Sun Bus, a sun slave who needs to be liberated, revolucion directo. I am a strange bird flying up, straight up into the great sun, my wings are yellow with it, they flame into it, the top of the pyramid spouts liquid gold, a gold volcano, floating me away on the wave of it. In the mirror of the sun I see my gold face, gold teeth and hair, I see sunflowers sprung up huge & turning with the sun, covering the sunburnt landscape from horizon to horizon, I hear sun adazzle through a silkscreen overlay, a near moon wings by, a Quetzalcoatl phoenix fills the upper air, dripping yellow sperm of light, there is no other paradise, there is no other consciousness, no other ecstacy, there is no death or dying, there is only change, there is only revolucion in the Territorio Libre of the Sun, there where the light pulses, the universe rings like a gong, I have discovered its tongue, light's clapper, there is no god but light in the flowerless fields, Territorio Libre del Sol where there is no god but life, but life turns out to be a Sonata in *Miao* Minor for an

Indifferent Cat, where Toltec strangers dance together
to a singing somewhere among the peyote blossoms
through which life freaks into being, the true timeless
life of ecstatic consciousness interrupted impromptu
now by US roman emperors of space in which my
skin dissolves and drifts away beyond the space-ship,
earth a very distant small blue ball lost in lonely time
disappearing now through a crystal crack. . . .

FERLING'ETTI

San Miguel

8 March '69

The policeman's traffic whistle in the dusk in the Plaza of San Miguel de Allende, sounding like hollow bird cries, the trees of the Jardin full of boat-tailed grackles, beautiful blackbirds crying out all at once in the last of the sunset, flocks of them swooping down upon the Jardin from other parts of town and crying out joyously (no other word for it) to the dying light. . . . The cooing of turtle-doves under far eaves. . . . The grackles in the Indian laurel and jacaranda trees, and the sound of armadillo guitars. . . . The Conchero dancers in the dusk under the jacarandas. . . . The Conchero dancers with armadillo guitars under the Indian laurels in front of La Parroquia. . . . The Aztec dancers with armadillo mandolins under the Indian laurels in the late dusk in front of the cathedral. . . . A tall young Indian prince, very bronze and very beautiful, with long bronze legs, dancing with an Indian maid in feathered headband, her eyes bloodshot. He plays his armadillo guitar as he dances, shellbells on his ankles. . . . A circle of older dancers surrounds them. They look in each others' eyes as they dance, unsmiling. A feather blows out of her headband into the center of the dancing circle where it lies on the cobbles. They dance around it, hooking their ankles together, slowly. They are smiling in each others' eyes, very beautiful. . . . The faint rattle and whir of their ankle bells, echoing hollowly, fills the sweet air.

10 Marzo '69

Lizards with flickering tongues on the broken stones
in the ruined gardens of Marfil. . . .

11 Marzo '69

Out at Atotonilco in the hot spring swimming pool
of a half-built resort, the "Incredible String Band"
(British) coming over the tape-recorder of some
butch gringos from New Jersey, the music blasting
out over the pool: "Through mangos, pomegranates,
and flames. . ." "There's a monkey coming to stay
tomorrow. What's that paraffin stove on your head?"
"I don't need a wife to lead the timeless life" "I'm
Buffalo Man, I'll do wrong as long as I can. . . ." A
mountain breeze blows & blows the willow trees.

12 Marzo '69

There's a story to be wondered about the roofless room in my semi-ruin of a house at 27 Recreo, San Miguel. A *criada* (a house maid) was killed in this room when the old wood & stone roof fell in a few years ago. (It's been cleared away now and at night in that room you can see the stars, pure & brilliant as through a wide telescope.) I don't know who was living here back then, nor whose *criada* she was, but I found the room at noon in blinding sunlight furnished only with four large, flat, square stones arranged in a square on the stone floor around a stone head with blue eyes. The sculptured stone is light grey, almost white, and it is the aquiline head of a young woman. The head is upright on a kind of altar-stone. High on the broken grey & mottled white plaster wall are two oval spots, each about two feet high, painted Indian red, resembling the high oval windows that let in light in some great rooms. I drew a face with closed eyes in each oval, and high up on another broken wall I hung an Indian God's Eye. . . . The room is about 20-feet-high, and the sun beats down directly into this room at noon as into some ruined temple. The stone head looks out into the fallen dry sunlight with its blue turquoise eyes, its speechless mouth half-open. Someone has stuck a thick, short, dark blue crayon between its lips. The sun slips behind a windy cloud somewhere and the sharp shadow of the head

disappears from the floor. The wind stirs a pile of dry green cocoa leaves in a corner. The sun comes out hot and burning again, and a brown hornet lights very slowly and drowzily on the lips of the silent woman, and she is the *criada,* with blue tongue, stoned to death. . . .

Saturday night, Marzo 15, '69

Barbarous night—At a party and some one passes me a pipe & I take several tokes & almost immediately find myself on a bad trip. First time that ever happened on Grass, I remember saying to myself, some one must have slipped me some shit; but every one around me had toked the same pipe, and there they all were, oblivious, sitting up in the semi-dark, watching color slides of Rembrandt in black stroboscopic light, laughing and grooving with it. Only it is super-stroboscopic to me. Rock on the recordplayer in the dark corner where I sit, and the whole room begins to rock, not only rock but move around sickeningly. I am in a cold sweat & feel the drops of it on my cold forehead. The room has closed in and I am trying to keep my mind working and then I zonk out completely. I am out for two or three minutes maybe and then I come to, gasping for air, people shaking me and asking in scared voices Am I OK? I say Yes, Yes, as if everything were normal, and someone hands me a plateful of spaghetti and brings me a glass of water. I can't hold them in my hands and I put them down on a low table so I won't drop them and a dude next to me says "He forgot to breathe, that happens sometimes. He's OK now." And everyone goes back to Rembrandt and rock, most of them stoned & oblivious; but I'm not OK, I'm

shivering and covered with cold perspiration, and I sit there in the semi-dark, trying to hold on to consciousness, trying not to zonk out again, calculating if I can make it out of the room to the fresh air, afraid if I get up I'll pass out en route. Rembrandts pulsate in the dark. What is happening? Someone turns up the music, who is someone, I begin to feel sick at my stomach and begin sweating again. I know I am going to throw up; but where, I have to get out at once, I do get out, somehow, threading my way through the bodies sitting strewn on the floor, leftovers from an experiential orgy, blocking the exit. I make it into the courtyard and keep going on out through the courtyard streetdoor, and as soon as I hit the dark cobbled street I throw up very violently, blah blah blah blah blah, leaning against a stone wall, wretching in the dark black, then stumble on down the narrowing, very dark street, homeward, missing a turn, going back, passing over a stone overpass, on up to the other end of town, better in fresh air but still in a cold sweat, still stoned stumbling a bit on the rough cobblestones, I remember everything, nothing, throwing up a few more times here and there en route in dark streets, thinking of "that great dark Thing—primitive Mexico" in black *pulque* night. . . . A couple groaning in a doorway, he into her, at it, heavy breath coming, coming. Blah. A *pulque* drunk lurches against me, white corn teeth gleaming under broken

sombrero, Indian eyes blind, glazed, primitive night
upon us, he in his dark world, I, mine; lurching past
each other, *almost* like lost humanoids, awful, beasts
abroad. Out of that alley and up "my" street, into my
door, unlock it, fall through it, into the veranda-court
under arches in moonlight, how calm all, how peace-
full, moonlight like white water filling up the court,
lapping. Light a candelabra, high up, rubber shadows
strumming, bullfrog gloat, crickets in a far place,
the moon is no angel, it only paints mescal freakscapes
I swim through, where is someone, the Mexican night
blots out silkscreen overlays of reptiles run through
an Osterizer, puree of brownjism bleached out, I walk
very quietly and slowly around the cloister in
moonlight, in silence, still high, afraid to lie down
and never wake again, walking and walking round
and round that square courtyard, by the ruined walls,
trying to come down, no place for a landing, air clears
my head, still up there, still high, trying not to
breathe or trying to breathe, so cold I put on a *jarongo,*
keep walking, fancy myself pulling myself together,
very funny dude in *serape,* stopped short and go to
bathroom, pee on funny wall through a silkscreen
underlay, catching looks at myself in dim mirror
hundred years olde, in my *jarongo,* Quetzalcoatl and
the fucking flapping Plumed Serpent, sperm prince
of darkness, the fairskinned blue-eyed "god" named
Lawrence come from across the sea to fuck the dark

peoples, a phoenix on my brow, I return to the cloister and continue walking flapping in *serape* around the square of it in broken moon, pieces of it falling off, there's a man on it turned reptile, fuck him, gringo man-in-moon waving plastic flag, I still here walking through the shadows of the great arches, still listening to the primitive night, crickets in it, somewhere, far off, I a strange bird flapping, wearing leather, creaking sandals. I keep creaking forward in them, I not Neal Cassady who died here in the rain at night along the railroad tracks, counting the ties to Celaya, this year, still high on life, he never walked but ran to wherever he was going, and so arrived there first, I not Neal whose lostandfound manuscreeds I'm here deciphering. . . .

All this had been going on a long time. And would go on. The night had no dawn attached to it. Or dawn had a lot of night still stuck to it, still hung on it, and couldn't get off the ground. The blackness, dark tar, pitch of night, black mescal, still stuck to everything. I had to be careful not to step on the lizards with flickering tongues in the cracks. I was still high. I couldn't come down. I kept walking. . . .

Baja Revisited

Sometime in time South of Rosarito— The Beach of
the Small Round Stones—when sea's rollers recede,
the round stones tumble over each other, with a
rumbling tumbling undersound, a deep clacking—
sea grinding its teeth. All night in the sea's jaws, under
the sea's roaring— Smoked some strong grass and fell
off into that roaring—the round stones like tumblers
in some great lock whirring around and tumbling at
last into place—sea and earth's great combination-
lock—"life's lock" fallen open— sea grinds its teeth
and moans *Ah,ah,ah*— I float on, a small island, made
of bodies attached by the lips, floating, hair streamed
out, body stretched out—"détendu"— Houses rise and
fall, with the tide. Morning beach in fog, scorpions
on the rocks, half-smoked "roaches"— the sun again
and sea's roar again over grey rocks, stretching away
miles on the Mexican strand—distant fisher figures on
it—and dried kelp, dried bulbous rubber sea tubes—"sea's
inner-tubes cast-up"—among bent beer cans, rusted
tongues alack, bleached white twigs, sea-flowers
cast up, dried stiff, all baked now in hot Mex sun—
"Never later in the memory will these flowers fade"—
Transcription of organ music—sea-tune to hurdygurdy
billion round small rocks, sea full of gulf streams,
floating all eternally away. . . . Golden field on distant
mountainside, "sending its signal to heaven". . . .

VW bus stuck in sand up to hub on right rear side—deserted beach at Colonia Guerrera, 60 miles South of Ensenada. Get it out finally by jacking up rear and putting rocks under wheel. "Could Purna Das fix a flat?" . . . . Got up in the 8 A. M. fog and addressed the sea—shaking my fist— "You— you— monster moitherer! Great groaner! Big blabbermouth, roiler and despoiler, roarer and rocker, you— you— talking asshole of the blithering world—you, world washer, eternal loudmouth and blabberer, cantor to the universe, answerer to Allen Ginsberg, om-singer & om-maker, you, blind, moithering, roistering, rabble-rouser! You, you, you mad monster flippy fric-frac faceless palaverer! Washer of the world's intestine, laver and looter of universe's underwear, death driver, life lighter, gargoyle-wave maker, salt bathtub of creation! Salter of sailors' wounds, embalmer of dead seagulls in sand, eternal embalmer, you, you stupid, ceaseless, slaphappy, shiftless shouter and shambler. You, intoner of Nothing! You, answerer of Nothing with Nothing! You, obscene old daddy sperm-spurter of them all, frothy foam-phallus of earth! Roaring and roaring all night! Crying Nothing! All! Alway! Never! Forever and ever! And ever! You!
Om! Fuck you! Fuck *you!*" . . . . Two silent waterbirds wing by, very close together, holding wingtips. . . . A huge dead seagull with wings outflung and bent back as if still hurtling down through air lies stiff on a dune, sandy wild beak still outstretched, empty

eye still fixed in skull, transfixed flat upon the sand
as upon a shield, emblematic, plumed serpent phoenix,
life . . . in the ocean's long withdrawing Om. . . .

Tiny, brilliant dark red sea-roses on the dunes,
just beyond reach of the sea–rasberry-like small red
roses, but made of sea-rubber, brilliant red amber &
green, glowing, in great low clusters, glistening
as diamonds. "Never later will these flowers fade. . . ."

Arrived just before nightfall at great wild white
sand beach ten miles South of San Quintín near San
Simon & Sky Ranch, over dirt roads running into
sand. . . . Bright red ball of sun down behind rugged
mountain promontory, great dunes hiding the roaring
ocean; and the VW bus gets back wheels stuck in
sand down to the hubs. Took a chance and raced
engine, and dug it in worse, so abandoned bus for the
night, took sleeping stuff & food & moved into
abandoned adobe shack, onto which had been added
an old trailer, with corrugated tin roof laid over old
adobe brown wall; inside, a big adobe fireplace with
metal hood and grates; and a porch made of sugarcane
stalks also covered by tin roof. . . . The beach: huge
sculpted hills of sand, sensuous, enormous breasts

of smooth, scalloped pure-white sand, each over twenty-feet-high, and these great forms running like immense waves from the shrub-ridge at top of beach to the sea itself, the whole width of beach at least 300 feet, stretching in both directions to bay horizons, sand scalloped hills casting long shadows as the red sun fell down into night. As if the mountains had allowed the wind to come through and make these shadows of themselves out of sand.

Walked through wild dunes to Rancho Santa Maria & got tractor to pull VW out, then settled in sugarcane shack on beach at Sta. Maria ($2 a night for the privilege) looking out over wide white beach, cobalt sea, succulent green seagrass, could be South Sea island, deep red sun falling down behind distant volcano-like mountain down the coast, in a sudden steep plunge, red fire sun absorbed in the black bold headland of mountain. . . . Woke to the seabirds' sound, cawing & crying over the dunes, far off. . . . One solitary small beach bird comes to perch on roof corner of grass shack & goes through his repertoire—a half-dozen different songs, or more, infinitely varied, trilling, calling, warbling, whistling—then flies away, not to return. . . Long lines of big silent fisher-birds wing in single formation low, over the dunes at water's edge, dipping to the waves, very slowly. . . .

And at the edge of a blowing meadow above a bluff,
three great white horses, *sitting*, looking out to sea,
motionless, white manes blowing in wind, each a
white bone statue, but alive, heads up, eyes fixed
forward in the wind, perfectly unmoving, under white
noon sun. . . . Two strange insects, two inches from
my nose where I lie on the beach alone, buzz and roll
over on each other, their many legs wrapped around
each other in a frenzy, making love or war, killing each
other or in trance-like rotor orgasm. It is love, not
death, and a warm wind blows; in a few seconds,
which could have been their eternity, one bug flings
itself off & goes straight away, fast, not looking back;
the other lies dazed, then moves slow in small circles,
no longer knowing where she is, if she ever did,
alone in a white sand land, stretching before & after. . . .

Curious how I hang on here, day after day, or is it
year after year, in my sugarcane shack on the dunes.
He who travels on peninsulas must expect someday
to turn back. It is as if I were waiting for the sea to
stop its absolute incoherence. . . . I see myself in the
dark distance, a stick-figure in the world's end. . . .

March 24, '69

La puerta escondida
                                        no es escondida
La puerta al invisible
                                        no es invisible
The door to the invisible
                                        is visible
The hidden door
                                   is not hidden
I continually walk through it
                                             not seeing it
And I am what I am
And will be what I will be
Sobre las playas perdidas
                                             del Sur. . . .

Books by Lawrence Ferlinghetti

Pictures of the Gone World
A Coney Island of the Mind
Her
Unfair Arguments with Existence
Routines
Starting from San Francisco
After the Cries of the Birds
The Secret Meaning of Things
Tyrannus Nix?
The Mexican Night: Travel Journal

The Mexican Night

—Travel Journal—